# Spud the Potato Bug

By Debbie Capiccioni (Heidinger)

Illustrated by Monique Turchan

Halo ●●●●
Publishing International

ISBN 13: 978-1-61244-017-0
Library of Congress Control Number: 2014908935

Printed in the United States of America

Halo Publishing International
www.halopublishing.com

Published by Halo Publishing International
AP·726
P.O. Box 60326
Houston, Texas 77205
Toll Free 1-877-705-9647
www.halopublishing.com
www.holapublishing.com
e-mail: contact@halopublishing.com

I would like to dedicate this book to my children and stepchildren. With that they gave me 15 grandchildren. Ryan, Jack, Carter, Nathan, Carmello, Malaya, Tessa, Ashley, Tayler, Breanna, Anthony, Leshaun, Corey, Emily and Robert. And to you Jonathan for a great portrait picture and so much dedication. Mom and Dad I wouldn't be here without you. Finally to my wonderful husband I love you infinity plus.

Sam always wondered how it would be.

To have a friend like you and me.

My friend you see is a potato bug.

I know he isn't something you hug.

But I do like playing with my bug.
Why a potato bug you say. I like the way
they roll that way.
He likes to roll into a ball.

That is when I like him most of all.

When I am done He goes to bed.

In a box where he likes to lay his head.

He isn't like any old bug.

His name is Spud the Potato bug.

I know a bug like Spud cannot be much fun.

But he is when you are the only one.

So alone I play like you and me.

With a bug named Spud so happily.

And through it all, he might be small.

To have a friend is the greatest gift of all.

CPSIA information can be obtained
at www.ICGtesting.com
Printed in the USA
BVXC01n0206050614
355391BV00009B/97

9 781612 440170